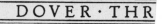

DOVER · THR

The Wit and Wisdom of Mark Twain

A Book of Quotations

MARK TWAIN

DOVER PUBLICATIONS, INC.
Mineola, New York

DOVER THRIFT EDITIONS

GENERAL EDITOR: PAUL NEGRI

Bibliographical Note

The Wit and Wisdom of Mark Twain: A Book of Quotations is a new work, first published by Dover Publications, Inc., in 1999. The quotations have been compiled from
various writings of Mark Twain.

Library of Congress Cataloging-in-Publication Data

Twain, Mark, 1835–1910.
    The wit and wisdom of Mark Twain : a book of quotations / Mark Twain.
        p.   cm. — (Dover thrift editions)
    ISBN 0-486-40664-4 (pbk.)
    1. Twain, Mark, 1835–1910 — Quotations. 2. Quotations, American. I. Title.
II. Series.
PS1303   1999
818'.409 — dc21   99-35832
                                                  CIP

Manufactured in the United States of America
Dover Publications, Inc., 31 East 2nd Street, Mineola, N.Y. 11501

Note

Mark Twain (Samuel Langhorne Clemens) has the dual distinction of being among America's most important writers and among its funniest. He was born in Florida, Missouri in 1835, and four years later moved to Hannibal, on the Mississippi River. As a young man he worked at a variety of jobs, including printer's typesetter and apprentice steamboat pilot (actually attaining a pilot's license in 1859), before heading West in search of fortune and adventure. After a stint as an unsuccessful prospector and miner, he began working as a journalist, and soon acquired a reputation as a humorous writer and lecturer specializing in tall tales and accounts of travel and adventure. His story "The Celebrated Jumping Frog of Calaveras County," published in a New York newspaper in 1865, was an instant classic of American humor. Over the next forty-five years, Twain wrote novels (including such classics as *The Adventures of Huckleberry Finn*), stories, essays, and sketches that earned him international fame and popularity and established him as a major figure in American literature. He died in 1910.

Twain traveled widely and saw much, and all that he saw was grist for his literary mill. He had an opinion about everything and a knack for expressing those opinions in such a pithy and memorable way that he became one of the most popular lecturers on both sides of the Atlantic. His humor ranges from the light-hearted to the bitterly ironic. The quotations in this book, taken from his novels, stories, essays, travel writings, letters and speeches, capture the essence of Twain's thought and style and are a source of wisdom and delight for anyone who reads them.

Contents

MEN, WOMEN, CHILDREN,
HUMAN NATURE

Man is the only animal that blushes. Or needs to.
"The Mysterious Stranger"

*

Man is the Reasoning Animal. Such is the claim.
I think it is open to dispute.   "The Lowest Animal"

*

Of all the animals, man is the only one that is
cruel. He is the only one that inflicts pain for the
pleasure of doing it.   "The Lowest Animal"

*

Man was made at the end of the week's work,
when God was tired.   Notebook

*

"The noblest work of God?" Man. "Who found it
out?" Man.

More Maxims of Mark, Merle Johnson, ed.

*

Man, "know thyself"— then thou wilt despise
thyself to a dead moral certainty.   Letter

Of course, no man is entirely in his right mind at any time.   "The Mysterious Stranger"

＊

No man has a wholly undiseased mind . . . in one way or another all men are mad.
                                        "The Memorable Assassination"

＊

When we remember we are all mad, the mysteries of life disappear and life stands explained.
                                                    Notebook

＊

The human race consists of the dangerously insane and such as are not.   Notebook

＊

The way it is now, the asylums can hold the sane people, but if we tried to shut up the insane we should run out of building materials.
                                        Following the Equator

＊

It is just like man's vanity and impertinence to call an animal dumb because it is dumb to his dull perceptions.   "What Is Man?"

＊

Circumstances make man, not man circumstances.   Notebook

The average man's a coward.
Adventures of Huckleberry Finn

*

The average human being is a perverse creature; and when he isn't that, he is a practical joker. The result to the other person concerned is about the same: that is, he is made to suffer.
Following the Equator

*

The timid man yearns for full value and asks a tenth. The bold man strikes for double value and compromises on par. *Following the Equator*

*

One never ceases to make a hero of one's self (in private). *The Gilded Age*

*

Clothes makes the man. Naked people have little or no influence in society.
More Maxims of Mark, Merle Johnson, ed.

*

However, we must put up without clothes as they are—they have their reason for existing. They are on us to expose us—to advertise what we wear them to conceal. *Following the Equator*

. . . man never does a single thing which has any first and foremost object except one—to secure peace of mind, spiritual comfort, for himself.

"What Is Man?"

*

There are many humorous things in the world; among them, the white man's notion that he is less savage than the other savages.

Following the Equator

*

There are no people who are quite so vulgar as the over-refined ones.   *Following the Equator*

*

She was not quite what you would call refined. She was not quite what you would call unrefined. She was the kind of person that keeps a parrot.

Following the Equator

*

If you pick up a starving dog and make him prosperous, he will not bite you. This is the principle difference between a dog and a man.

Pudd'nhead Wilson

*

Concerning the difference between man and the jackass: some observers hold that there isn't any. But this wrongs the jackass.   Notebook

When a man can prove that he is not a jackass, I think he is in the way to prove that he is no legitimate member of the race.   Letter

*

Such is the human race. Often it does seem such a pity that Noah didn't miss the boat.

Christian Science

*

Damn these human beings; if I had invented them I would go hide my head in a bag.   Letter

*

I am only human, although I regret it.

Mark Twain's Autobiography, Albert Bigelow Paine, ed.

*

Adam and Eve had many advantages, but the principle one was that they escaped teething.

Pudd'nhead Wilson

*

[On woman] As a sweetheart, she has few equals and no superiors; as a cousin, she is convenient; as a wealthy grandmother with an incurable distemper, she is precious; as a wet-nurse, she has no equal among men.   "Woman—An Opinion" (speech)

*

What, sir, would the people of the earth be without woman? They would be scarce, sir, almighty scarce.   "Woman—An Opinion" (speech)

Some civilized women would lose half their charm without dress; and some would lose all of it.
                    "Woman, God Bless Her!" (speech)

*

One frequently only finds out how really beautiful a beautiful woman is after considerable acquaintance with her.   *The Innocents Abroad*

*

Slang in a woman's mouth is not obscene, it only sounds so.
                    More Maxims of Mark, Merle Johnson, ed.

*

There is only one good sex. The female one.
                    Attributed

*

Heroine: girl who is perfectly charming to live with, in a book.
                    More Maxims of Mark, Merle Johnson, ed.

*

It takes much to convince the average man of anything; and perhaps nothing can ever make him realize that he is the average woman's inferior.
                    Following the Equator

*

No civilization can be perfect until exact equality between man and woman is included.   Notebook

The phases of the womanly nature are infinite in their variety. Take any type of woman, and you will find in it something to respect, something to admire, something to love.   "The Ladies" (speech)

*

Nothing is so ignorant as a man's left hand, except a lady's watch.   *Following the Equator*

*

Familiarity breeds contempt—and children.
                                        Notebook

*

We lavish gifts upon them [children]; but the most precious gift—our personal association, which means so much to them—we give grudgingly.
          Mark Twain: A Biography, Albert Bigelow Paine

•

As long as you're in your right mind don't you ever pray for twins. Twins amount to a permanent riot. And there ain't any real difference between triplets and an insurrection.   "The Babies" (speech)

*

A baby is an inestimable blessing and bother.
                                        Letter

LOVE, MARRIAGE, ROMANCE

After all these years, I see that I was mistaken about Eve in the beginning; it is better to live outside the Garden with her than inside it without her.
"Adam's Diary"

*

When you fish for love, bait with your heart, not your brain.   Notebook

*

You can't reason with your heart; it has its own laws and thumps about things which the intellect scorns.   *A Connecticut Yankee in King Arthur's Court*

*

No woman or man really knows what perfect love is until they have been married a quarter of a century.   Notebook

*

Marriage—yes, it is the supreme felicity of life. I concede it. And it is also the supreme tragedy of life. The deeper the love, the surer the tragedy.   Letter

*

Both marriage and death ought to be welcome: the one promises happiness, doubtless the other assures it.   Letter

*

Some of us cannot be optimists, but all of us can be bigamists.
More Maxims of Mark, Merle Johnson, ed.

VIRTUE, VICE, CONDUCT

Always do right. This will gratify some people, and astonish the rest.

Note to Young People's Society

*

Do right and you will be conspicuous.

Mark Twain: A Biography, Albert Bigelow Paine

*

A man should not be without morals; it is better to have bad morals than none at all.   Notebook

*

Be good and you will be lonesome.

Following the Equator

*

Do your duty today and repent tomorrow.

More Maxims of Mark, Merle Johnson, ed.

*

To be good is to be noble; but to show others how to be good is nobler and no trouble.

Following the Equator

*

Morals are an acquirement—like music, like a foreign language, like piety, poker, paralysis—no man is born with them.

"Seventieth Birthday" (speech)

Morals consist of political morals, commercial morals, ecclesiastical morals, and morals.
                    More Maxims of Mark, Merle Johnnson, ed.

                              *

It is not best that we use our morals week days; it gets them out of repair for Sundays.   Notebook

                              *

Better a broken promise than none at all.
                    More Maxims of Mark, Merle Johnson, ed.

                              *

Get your formalities right—never mind about the moralities.   *Following the Equator*

                              *

Virtue never has been as respectable as money.
                    The Innocents Abroad

                              *

· Do good when you can, and charge when you think they will stand it.
                    More Maxims of Mark, Merle Johnson, ed.

                              *

There is a Moral Sense and there is an Immoral Sense. History shows us that the Moral Sense enables us to perceive morality and how to avoid it, and that the Immoral Sense enables us to perceive immorality and how to enjoy it.
                    Following the Equator

Few things are harder to put up with than the annoyance of a good example.   *Pudd'nhead Wilson*

*

Nothing so needs reforming as other people's habits.   *Pudd'nhead Wilson*

*

A man may have no bad habits and have worse.
          Following the Equator

*

We can secure other people's approval, if we do right and try hard; but our own is worth a hundred of it, and no way has been found out of securing that.   *Following the Equator*

*

We ought never to do wrong when people are looking.   "A Double-Barreled Detective Story"

*

Always obey your parents, when they are present. This is the best policy in the long run, because if you don't they will make you.
          "Advice to Youth" (speech)

*

Yes, always avoid violence. In this age of charity and kindliness, the time has gone by for such things. Leave dynamite to the low and unrefined.
          "Advice to Youth" (speech)

There's a good spot tucked away somewhere in everybody. You'll be a long time finding it sometimes.   "Refuge of the Derelicts"

*

Everyone is a moon, and has a dark side which he never shows to anyone.   *Following the Equator*

*

Nothing incites to money-crimes like great poverty or great wealth.
          More Maxims of Mark, Merle Johnson, ed.

*

Adam was the author of sin, and I wish he had taken out an international copyright on it.
                                        Notebook

*

A sin takes on new and real terrors when there seems a chance that it is going to be found out.
          "The Man That Corrupted Hadleyburg"

*

Martyrdom covers a multitude of sins.
                                        Notebook

*

To lead a life of undiscovered sin! That is true joy.
          "My Real Self" (speech)

The more things are forbidden, the more popular they become.   Notebook

*

[Adam] did not want the apple for the apple's sake, he wanted it only because it was forbidden. The mistake was in not forbidding the serpent; then he would have eaten the serpent.

Pudd'nhead Wilson

*

[Adam] A man who comes down to us without a stain upon his name, unless it was a stain to take one apple when most of us would have taken the whole crop.   "On Adam" (speech)

*

To promise not to do a thing is the surest way in the world to make a body want to go and do that very thing.   *Tom Sawyer*

*

Earn a character first if you can. And if you can't assume one.   "General Miles and the Dog" (speech)

*

Make it a point to do something every day that you don't want to do. This is the golden rule for acquiring the habit of doing your duty without pain.

Following the Equator

... in order to make a man or a boy covet a thing, it is only necessary to make the thing difficult to attain.   *Tom Sawyer*

*

Always acknowledge a fault frankly. This will throw those in authority off guard and give you an opportunity to commit more.   Notebook

*

One mustn't criticize other people on grounds where he can't stand perpendicular himself.
          A *Connecticut Yankee in King Arthur's Court*

*

I haven't a particle of confidence in a man who has no redeeming petty vices whatever.
          Mark Twain: A Biography, Albert Bigelow Paine

*

An uneasy conscience is a hair in the mouth.
          Notebook

*

It [conscience] takes up more room than all the rest of a person's insides.   *Huckleberry Finn*

*

The idea of a *civil* conscience! It is a good joke; an excellent joke. All the consciences I have ever heard of were nagging, badgering, fault-finding, execrable savages!   "Crime Carnival in Connecticut"

There are several good protections against temptations but the surest is cowardice.

Following the Equator

⁕

Courage is resistance to fear, mastery of fear, not absence of fear.

Puddn'head Wilson

⁕

There are not enough morally brave men in stock. We are out of moral-courage material. . . .

"The United States of Lyncherdom"

⁕

To believe yourself brave is to be brave.

Joan of Arc

⁕

It is better to deserve honors and not have them than to have them and not deserve them.

Notebook

⁕

If any man has just merciful and kindly instincts he would be a gentleman, for he would need nothing else in the world. "Layman's Sermon" (speech)

⁕

When people do not respect us we are sharply offended; yet in his private heart no man much respects himself.

Following the Equator

Human pride is not worth while; there is always
something lying in wait to take the wind out of it.
Following the Equator

*

I was born modest; not all over, but in spots.
A Connecticut Yankee in King Arthur's Court

*

The man who is ostentatious of his modesty is
twin to the statue that wears a fig-leaf.
Following the Equator

*

By trying, we can easily learn to endure adversity.
Another man's, I mean.   *Following the Equator*

*

Man will do many things to get himself loved, he
will do all things to get himself envied.
Following the Equator

*

The universal brotherhood of man is our most
precious possession, what there is of it.
Following the Equator

*

If a person offends you and you are in doubt as to
whether it was intentional or not, do not resort to ex-
treme measures. Simply watch your chance and hit
him with a brick.   "Advice to Youth" (speech)

A human being has a natural desire to have more of a good thing than he needs.

Following the Equator

*

It is not best that we should all think alike; it is difference of opinion that makes horse races.

Pudd'nhead Wilson

*

A crime preserved in a thousand centuries ceases to be a crime, and becomes a virtue. This is the law of custom, and custom supersedes all other forms of law.   *Following the Equator*

*

Gratitude and treachery are merely the two extremities of the same procession. You have seen all of it that is worth staying for when the band and the gaudy officials have gone by.   *Pudd'nhead Wilson*

*

Diligence is a good thing, but taking things easy is much more—restful.   "Business" (speech)

*

Loyalty to petrified opinions never yet broke a chain or freed a human soul.   "Consistency"

*

There is no character, howsoever good and fine, but it can be destroyed by ridicule, howsoever poor and witless.   *Pudd'nhead Wilson*

The secret source of humor itself is not joy but sorrow. There is no humor in heaven.
Following the Equator

*

Chastity—it can be carried too far.
"Andrew Carnegie" (speech)

*

Modesty died when clothes were born.
Mark Twain: A Biography, Albert Bigelow Paine

*

Each race determines for itself what indecencies are. Nature knows no indecencies; man invents them.   Notebook

*

When angry, count four; when very angry, swear.
Pudd'nhead Wilson

*

We begin to swear before we can talk.
Following the Equator

*

If the desire to kill and the opportunity to kill came always together, who would escape hanging?
Following the Equator

In certain trying circumstances, urgent circumstances, desperate circumstances, profanity furnishes a relief denied even to prayer.
Mark Twain: A Biography, Albert Bigelow Paine

*

Grief can take care of itself; but to get the full value of a joy you must have somebody to divide it with.   *Following the Equator*

*

Be careless in your dress if you must, but keep a tidy soul.   *Following the Equator*

*

Let us endeavor so to live that when we come to die even the undertaker will be sorry.
Pudd'nhead Wilson

POLITICS, HISTORY

Prosperity is the best protector of principle.
Following the Equator

*

Principles have no real force except when one is well fed.   "Adam's Diary"

*

We all live in the protection of certain cowardices which we call our principles.
More Maxims of Mark, Merle Johnson, ed.

Irreverence is the champion of liberty and its only sure defense.   Notebook

*

. . . no people in the world ever did achieve freedom by goody-goody talk and moral suasion: it being immutable law that all revolutions that will succeed must *begin* in blood.
                    A *Connecticut Yankee in King Arthur's Court*

*

It is by the goodness of God that in our country we have those three unspeakably precious things: freedom of speech, freedom of conscience, and the prudence never to practice either of them.
                    Following the Equator

*

We are called the nation of inventors. And we are. We could still claim that title and wear its loftiest honors if we had stopped with the first thing we ever invented—which was human liberty.
                    "On Foreign Critics" (speech)

*

We have a criminal jury system which is superior to any in the world; and its efficiency is only marred by the difficulty of finding twelve men every day who don't know anything and can't read.
                    "Americans and the English" (speech)

Trial by jury is the palladium of our liberties. I do not know what a palladium is, having never seen a palladium, but it is a good thing no doubt at any rate.
                                                        Roughing It

*

That's the difference between governments and individuals. Governments don't care, individuals do.
                                                        A Tramp Abroad

*

A nation is only an individual multiplied.
                                        "The Turning-Point of My Life"

*

There are written laws—they perish; but there are also unwritten laws—they are eternal.
                        A Connecticut Yankee in King Arthur's Court

*

My kind of loyalty was loyalty to one's country, not to its institutions or its office-holders.
                        A Connecticut Yankee in King Arthur's Court

*

The radical of one century is the conservative of the next. The radical invents the views; when he has worn them out the conservative adopts them.
                                                        Notebook

To arrive at a just estimate of a renowned man's character one must judge it by the standards of his time, not ours.   *Joan of Arc*

*

To be vested with enormous authority is a fine thing; but to have the onlooking world consent to it is a finer.
        A *Connecticut Yankee in King Arthur's Court*

*

A historian who would convey the truth has got to lie.   *Mark Twain: A Biography*, Albert Bigelow Paine

*

The very ink with which all history is written is merely fluid prejudice.   *Following the Equator*

*

Where every man has a vote, brutal laws are impossible. A *Connecticut Yankee in King Arthur's Court*

*

Citizenship is what makes a republic; monarchies can get along without it. What keeps a republic on its legs is good citizenship.
                "Layman's Sermon" (speech)

*

All I say is kings is kings, and you got to make allowances. Take them all around, they're a mighty ornery lot. It's the way they're raised.
                Adventures of Huckleberry Finn

The kingly office is entitled to no respect. It was originally procured by the highwayman's methods; it remains a perpetuated crime, can never be anything but the symbol of a crime.   Notebook

*

This atrocious doctrine of allegiance to party plays directly into the hands of politicians of the baser sort—and doubtless for that it was borrowed—or stolen—from the monarchical system.

"Consistency" (speech)

*

This nation is like all the others that have been spewed upon the earth—ready to shout for any cause that will tickle its vanity or fill its pocket. What a hell of a heaven it will be when they get all these hypocrites assembled there!   Letter

*

It could probably be shown by facts and figures that there is no distinctly native American criminal class except Congress.   *Following the Equator*

*

Suppose you were an idiot. And suppose you were a member of Congress. But I repeat myself.
Mark Twain: A Biography, Albert Bigelow Paine

*

Fleas can be taught nearly anything that a Congressman can.   "What Is Man?"

Demagogue—a vessel containing beer and other liquids.   "Girls" (speech)

RELIGION

[Man] is the only animal that has the True Religion—several of them.   "The Lowest Animal"

*

The Christian Bible is a drug store. Its contents remain the same; but the medical practice changes.
"Bible Teaching and Religious Practice"

*

If a man doesn't believe as we do, we say he is a crank, and that settles it. I mean it does nowadays, because now we can't burn him.
Following the Equator

*

There has been only one Christian. They caught and crucified him—early.   Notebook

*

There are two kinds of Christian morals, one private and the other public. These two are so distinct, so unrelated, that they are no more akin to each other than are archangels and politicians.
"Taxes and Morals" (speech)

Two or three centuries from now it will be recognized that all the competent killers are Christians; then the pagan world will go to school to the Christian—not to acquire his religion, but his guns.

"The Mysterious Stranger"

*

Monarchies, aristocracies, and religions are all based upon that large defect in your race—the individual's distrust of his neighbor, and his desire, for safety's or comfort's sake, to stand well in his neighbor's eye.   "The Mysterious Stranger"

*

... tyrannical, murderous, rapacious, and morally rotten as they [the nobility] were, they were deeply and enthusiastically religious.

A Connecticut Yankee in King Arthur's Court

*

The church is always trying to get other people to reform; it might not be a bad idea to reform itself a little by way of example.   A Tramp Abroad

*

The Church has opposed every innovation and discovery from the day of Galileo down to our own time, when the use of Anesthetics in childbirth was regarded as a sin because it avoided the biblical curse pronounced against Eve.

Mark Twain: A Biography, Albert Bigelow Paine

Religion had its share in the changes of civilization and national character, of course. What share? The lion's.	"Bible Teaching and Religious Practice"

*

[The preacher] never charged nothing for his preaching, and it was worth it, too.
Adventures of Huckleberry Finn

*

There are those who scoff at the schoolboy, calling him frivolous and shallow. Yet it was the schoolboy who said "Faith is believing what you know ain't so."	*Following the Equator*

*

There is nothing more awe-inspiring than a miracle except the credulity that can take it at par.
Notebook

*

The proverb says that Providence protects children and idiots. This is really true. I know it because I have tested it.
Mark Twain's Autobiography, Albert Bigelow Paine, ed.

*

The first thing a missionary teaches a savage is indecency.	Notebook

*

True irreverence is disrespect for another man's god.	Notebook

In God We Trust. I don't believe it would sound any better if it were true.   Notebook

*

God's inhumanity to man makes countless thousands mourn.   Notebook

*

The book of nature tells us distinctly that God cares not a rap for us—nor for any living creature.
                                                         Notebook

*

Eternal Rest sounds comforting in the pulpit . . . Well, you try it once, and see how heavy time will hang on your hands.
                    "Captain Stormfield's Visit to Heaven"

*

Let me make the superstitions of a nation and I care not who makes its laws.   *Following the Equator*

*

India has two million gods, and worships them all. In religion other countries are paupers; India is the only millionaire.   *Following the Equator*

*

One of the proofs of the immortality of the soul is that myriads have believed in it. They have also believed the world was flat.   Notebook

When I reflect upon the number of disagreeable people who I know have gone to a better world, I am moved to lead a different life.

Pudd'nhead Wilson

*

Heaven for climate, Hell for company.

Notebook

*

If I cannot swear in heaven I shall not stay there.

Notebook

YOUTH, AGING

When I was a boy of of fourteen, my father was so ignorant I could hardly stand to have the old man around. But when I got to be twenty-one, I was astonished at how much he had learned in seven years.   Attributed

*

It is a wise child that knows its own father, and an unusual one that unreservedly approves of him.

More Maxims of Mark, Merle Johnson, ed.

*

There is no sadder sight than a young pessimist.

Notebook

The man who is a pessimist before 48 knows too much; if he is an optimist after it, he knows too little.   *Mark Twain: A Biography*, Albert Bigelow Paine

*

At 50 a man can be an ass without being an optimist but not an optimist without being an ass.
                    More Maxims of Mark, Merle Johnson, ed.

*

Pessimist: the optimist who didn't arrive.
                    More Maxims of Mark, Merle Johnson, ed.

*

Wrinkles should merely indicate where smiles have been.   *Following the Equator*

*

Twenty-four years ago I was strangely handsome. The remains of it are still visible through the rifts of time.   Letter

*

Why, she [Sarah Bernhardt] is the youngest person I ever saw, except myself—for I always feel young when I come in the presence of young people.   "Russian Sufferers" (speech)

*

Whatever a man's age, he can reduce it several years by putting a bright-colored flower in his button hole.   *The American Claimant*

Consider well the proportions of things. It is better to be a young June-bug than an old bird of paradise.   *Pudd'nhead Wilson*

*

We have no permanent habits until we are forty. Then they begin to harden, presently they petrify, then business begins.

"Seventieth Birthday" (speech)

*

And I urge upon you this—which I think is wisdom—if you find you can't make seventy by any but an uncomfortable road, don't you go.

"Seventieth Birthday" (speech)

*

I have achieved my seventy years in the usual way: by sticking strictly to a scheme of life which would kill anybody else.

"Seventieth Birthday" (speech)

*

Life should begin with age and its privileges and accumulations, and end with youth and its capacity to splendidly enjoy such advantages. . . . It's an epitome of life. The first half of it consists of the capacity to enjoy without the chance. The last half consists of the chance without the capacity.   Letter

*

What is human life? The first third a good time; the rest remembering about it.

More Maxims of Mark, Merle Johnson, ed.

We should be careful to get out of an experience only the wisdom that is in it—and stop there; lest we be like the cat that sits down on a hot stove-lid. She will never sit down on a hot stove-lid again—and that is well; but also she will never sit down on a cold one anymore. *Following the Equator*

*

Whoever has lived long enough to find out what life is, knows how deep a debt of gratitude we owe to Adam, the first great benefactor of our race. He brought death into the world. *Pudd'nhead Wilson*

*

Death, the refuge, the solace, the best and kindliest and most prized friend and benefactor of the erring, the forsaken, the old, and weary, and broken of heart, whose burdens be heavy upon them, and who would lie down and be at rest.

"On Adam" (speech)

*

All say, "How hard it is that we have to die"—a strange complaint to come from the mouths of people who have had to live. *Pudd'nhead Wilson*

TRUTH, HONESTY, LIES, ILLUSION

When in doubt tell the truth.

Following the Equator

*

Tell the truth or trump—but get the trick.

Pudd'nhead Wilson

Truth is the most valuable thing we have. Let us economize it.   *Following the Equator*

*

I don't mind what the opposition say of me so long as they don't tell the truth about me.
                    Republican Rally speech

*

Truth is good manners; manners are a fiction.
                    "The Mysterious Stranger"

*

Often the surest way to convey misinformation is to tell the strict truth.   *Following the Equator*

*

Truth is stranger than fiction, but it is because fiction is obliged to stick to possibilities; Truth isn't.
                    Following the Equator

*

No real gentleman will tell the naked truth in the presence of the ladies.
                    "A Double-Barreled Detective Story"

*

Barring that natural expression of villainy which we all have, the man looked honest enough.
                    "A Mysterious Visit"

Yes, even I am dishonest. Not in many ways, but in some. Forty-one, I think.   Letter

*

There are people who believe that honesty is always the best policy. This is a superstition; there are times when the appearance of it are worth six of it.
                    Following the Equator

*

Honesty is the best policy—when there is money in it.   "Business" (speech)

*

Some people lie when they tell the truth. I tell the truth lying.   Interview

*

I never could tell a lie that anyone would doubt, nor a truth that anybody would believe.
                    Following the Equator

*

I am not one of those who in expressing opinions confine themselves to facts. I don't know anything that mars good literature so completely as too much truth.   "The Savage Club Dinner" (speech)

*

Carlyle said "a lie cannot live." It shows that he did not know how to tell them.
Mark Twain's Autobiography, Albert Bigelow Paine, ed.

An honest man in politics shines more than he would elsewhere.   *A Tramp Abroad*

＊

As by the fire of experience, so by commission of crime, you learn real morals.
          "Theoretical and Practical Morals" (speech)

＊

Reputation is a hallmark. It can remove doubt from pure silver and it can also make the plated article pass for pure. And so people without a hallmark of their own are always trying to get the loan of somebody's else's.   Letter

＊

Don't part with your illusions. When they are gone you may still exist, but you have ceased to live.
                    Following the Equator

＊

He had arrived at the point where presently the illusions would cease and he would have entered upon the realities of life, and God help the man that has arrived at that point.   "Joan of Arc" (speech)

＊

Against a diseased imagination, demonstration goes for nothing.   "A Campaign That Failed"

＊

Many a small thing has been made large by advertising.
          A Connecticut Yankee in King Arthur's Court

You want to be very careful about lying; otherwise you are nearly sure to get caught.

"Advice to Youth" (speech)

*

It is often the case that a man who can't tell a lie thinks he is the best judge of one.

Pudd'nhead Wilson's Calendar

*

A lie can travel halfway around the world while the truth is putting on its shoes.   Attributed

*

One of the striking differences between a cat and a lie it that a cat has only nine lives.

Pudd'nhead Wilson

*

A truth is not hard to kill . . . a lie told well is immortal.   "Advice to Youth" (speech)

*

An awkward, feeble, leaky lie is a thing which you ought to make it your unceasing study to avoid; such a lie as that has no more real permanence than an average truth.   "Advice to Youth" (speech)

*

There are 869 different forms of lying, but only one of them has been squarely forbidden. Thou shalt not bear false witness against they neighbor.

Following the Equator

The old saw says "Let a sleeping dog lie." Still, when there is much at stake it is better to get a newspaper to do it.   *Following the Equator*

READING, WRITING, EDUCATION

A classic—something that everybody wants to have read and nobody wants to read.
            "The Disappearance of Literature" (speech)

*

"Classic." A book which people praise and don't read.   *Following the Equator*

*

If books are not good company, where will I find it?   Letter

*

A successful book is not made of what is in it, but what is left out of it.   Letter

*

Imagination labors best in distant fields.
                                    The Innocents Abroad

*

War talk by men who have been in a war is always interesting; whereas moon talk by a poet who has not been in the moon is likely to be dull.
                                    Life on the Mississippi

Pilgrim's Progress, about a man that left his family, it didn't say why.   *Huckleberry Finn*

*

[James Fenimore Cooper's] *Deerslayer* is just simply a literary *delirium tremens*.
            "Fenimore Cooper's Literary Offenses"

*

The fact of the business is, you've got to be one of two ages to appreciate [Walter] Scott. When you're eighteen you can read *Ivanhoe*, and you want to wait until you are ninety to read some of the rest.
            "The Disappearance of Literature" (speech)

*

I can't stand George Eliot and Hawthorne and those people. I see what they are at a hundred years before they get to it and they just tire me to death.
                                                Letter

*

As for *The Bostonians* [by Henry James] , I would rather be damned to John Bunyan's heaven than read that.   Letter

*

Also, to be fair, there is another word of praise due to this ship's library: it contains no copy of [Oliver Goldsmith's] *The Vicar of Wakefield* . . . a book which is one long waste-pipe discharge of goody-goody puerilities and dreary moralities. . . .
                                    Following the Equator

Jane Austen's books, too, are absent from this library. Just that one omission alone would make a fairly good library out of a library that hadn't a book in it.   *Following the Equator*

*

Tom Sawyer is simply a hymn put into prose form to give it a worldly air.   Letter

*

Persons attempting to find a motive in this narrative will be prosecuted; persons attempting to find a moral in it will be banished; persons attempting to find a plot in it will be shot.
          "Notice" in *Adventures of Huckleberry Finn*

*

They [the Concord, Mass. Library] have expelled Huck from their library as "trash and suitable only for the slums." That will sell 25,000 copies for us sure.   Letter

*

To my mind, that literature is best and most enduring which is characterized by a noble simplicity.
                    "Montreal Address" (speech)

*

The humorous story is American, the comic story is English, the witty story is French. The humorous story depends for its effect upon the manner of the telling; the comic story and the witty story on the matter.   "How to Tell a Story"

Perhaps no poet is a conscious plagiarist; but there seems to be warrant for suspecting that there is no poet who is not at one time or another an unconscious one.   *Following the Equator*

*

The library at the British Museum I find particularly astounding. I have read there hours together, and hardly made an impression on it.

"About London" (speech)

*

There is no such thing as "the Queen's English." The property has gone into the hands of a joint stock company and we own the bulk of the shares!

Following the Equator

*

There are many sorts of books; but good ones are the sort for the young to read.

"Advice to Youth" (speech)

*

It seems to me that just in the ratio that our newspapers increase, our morals decay.

"License of the Press" (speech)

*

He was as shy as a newspaper is when referring to its own merits.   *Following the Equator*

That awful power, the public opinion of a nation, is created in America by a horde of ignorant, self-complacent simpletons who failed at ditching and shoemaking and fetched up in journalism on their way to the poorhouse.

"License of the Press" (speech)

*

A man is always better than his printed opinions.

"Hamilton W. Mabie" (speech)

*

My works are like water. The works of the great masters are like wine. But everyone drinks water.

Notebook

*

In writing plays the chief thing is novelty. The world grows tired of solid forms in all the arts.

"Henry Irving" (speech)

*

As to the adjective: when in doubt, strike it out.

Pudd'nhead Wilson

*

It is more trouble to make a maxim than to do right.   *Following the Equator*

*

It is noble to teach oneself, but still nobler to teach others—and less trouble.

"Doctor Van Dyke" (speech)

It is better to support schools than jails.
"Feeding a Dog on Its Own Tail" (speech)

*

We believe that out of the public school grows the greatness of a nation.
"Public Education Association " (speech)

*

Everything has its limit—iron ore cannot be educated into gold.
"What Is Man?"

*

Training is everything . . . cauliflower is nothing but cabbage with a college education.
Pudd'nhead Wilson

*

Education consists mainly in what we have unlearned.
Notebook

*

In the first place God made idiots. This was for practice. Then he made school boards.
Following the Equator

HEALTH, EXERCISE

The only way to keep your health is to eat what you don't want, drink what you don't like, and do what you'd druther not.
Following the Equator

I have never taken any exercise, except sleeping and resting, and I never intend to take any. Exercise is loathsome. And it cannot be any benefit when you are tired; and I was always tired.

"Seventieth Birthday" (speech)

*

Do not undervalue the headache. While it is at its sharpest it seems a bad investment; but when relief begins the unexpired remainder is worth $4.00 a minute. *Following the Equator*

*

In the matter of diet I have been persistently strict in sticking to the things which didn't agree with me until one or the other of us got the best of it.

"Seventieth Birthday" (speech)

*

I always take it [Scotch whisky] at night as a preventive of toothache. I have never had the toothache; and what is more, I never intend to have it.

Europe and Elsewhere

*

Taking the pledge will not make bad liquor good, but it will improve it.

More Maxims of Mark, Merle Johnson, ed.

*

Temperate temperance is best.   Notebook

*

I have made it a rule never to smoke more than one cigar at a time.   "Seventieth Birthday" (speech)

MONEY, BUSINESS

There are two times in a man's life when he should not speculate: when he can't afford it, and when he can. *Following the Equator*

*

My axiom is, to succeed in business: avoid my example. "Business" (speech)

*

He is now fast rising from affluence to poverty.
"Henry Ward Beecher's Farm"

*

Simple rules for saving money: To save half, when you are fired by an eager impulse to contribute to a charity, wait, and count forty. To save three-quarters, count sixty. To save it all, count sixty-five. *Following the Equator*

*

The lack of money is the root of all evil.
More Maxims of Mark, Merle Johnson, ed.

*

There is nothing more beneficent than accident insurance. I have seen an entire family lifted out of poverty and into affluence by the simple boon of a broken leg. "Accident Insurance" (speech)

TRAVEL

I have found out that there ain't no surer way to
find out whether you like people or hate them than
to travel with them.   *Tom Sawyer Abroad*

*

The gentle reader will never know what a con-
summate ass he can become until he goes abroad.
                                        The Innocents Abroad

*

The average man is profoundly ignorant of countries that lie remote from his own.
                                        Following the Equator

*

Travel is fatal to prejudice, bigotry, and narrow-
mindedness, and many of our people need it sorely
on these accounts.   *The Innocents Abroad*

*

The Creator made Italy with designs by
Michelangelo.   *The Innocents Abroad*

*

There are several "sights" in the Bermudas, of
course, but they are easily avoided. This is a great
advantage—one cannot have it in Europe.
                                   "Notes of an Idle Excursion"

*

Nothing helps scenery like bacon and eggs.
                                              Roughing It

They spell it Vinci and pronounce it vinchy; for-
eigners always spell better than they pronounce.

The Innocents Abroad

*

These natives are strange people—they can die
whenever they want to—don't mind dying anymore
than a jilted Frenchman.

"The Sandwich Islands" (speech)

*

The Germans are exceedingly fond of Rhine
wines; they are put up in tall, slender bottles, and
are considered a pleasant beverage. One tells them
from vinegar by the label.   *A Tramp Abroad*

*

[On London Family Hotels] They are a London
specialty. God has not permitted them to exist elsewhere. . . . All the modern inconveniences are
furnished, and some that have been obsolete for a
century. The bedrooms are hospitals for incurable
furniture.   Letter

*

It used to be a good hotel, but that proves nothing—I used to be a good boy.

The Innocents Abroad

*

I have seen all the foreign countries I want to see
except heaven and hell, and I have only a vague cu-
riosity as concerns one of those.   Letter

VARIOUS SUBJECTS

The reports of my death are greatly exaggerated.
　　　　　　　　　　　　　　　　　Cablegram

*

I am used to swan songs; I have sung them several
times.　　　　　　　　　"Seventieth Birthday" (speech)

*

The cross of the Legion of Honor has been
conferred upon me. However, few escape that
distinction.　　　　　　　　　　*A Tramp Abroad*

*

I have been on the verge of being an angel all my
life, but it's never happened yet.
　　　Mark Twain: A Biography, Albert Bigelow Paine

*

I was always heedless. I was born heedless; and
therefore I was constantly, and quite unconsciously,
committing breaches of the minor proprieties,
which brought upon me humiliations which ought
to have humiliated me but didn't, because I didn't
know anything had happened.
　　Mark Twain's Autobiography, Albert Bigelow Paine, ed.

*

It takes me a long time to lose my temper, but
once lost I could not find it with a dog.　　Notebook

It is the little conveniences that make the real comfort of life.

> A *Connecticut Yankee in King Arthur's Court*

*

Habit is habit, and not to be flung out of the window by any man, but coaxed downstairs a step at a time.   *Pudd'nhead Wilson*

*

Custom makes incongruous things congruous.

> *Following the Equator*

*

To be busy is man's only happiness.   Letter

*

The exercise of an extraordinary gift is the supremest pleasure in life.   *The American Claimant*

*

Do not put off till tomorrow what can be put off till day-after-tomorrow just as well.

> *More Maxims of Mark*, Merle Johnson, ed.

*

There are people who can do all fine and heroic things except one! keep from telling their happiness to the unhappy.   *Following the Equator*

Each person is born to one possession which out-values all his others—his last breath.

Following the Equator

*

Why is it that we rejoice at a birth and grieve at a funeral? It is because we are not the person involved. *Pudd'nhead Wilson*

*

The Autocrat of Russia possesses more power than any other man in the earth; but he cannot stop a sneeze. *Following the Equator*

*

There isn't a Parallel of latitude but thinks it would have been the Equator if it had had its rights.

Following the Equator

*

The English are mentioned in the Bible; Blessed are the meek, for they shall inherit the earth.

Following the Equator

*

Against the assault of laughter nothing can stand.

"The Mysterious Stranger"

*

The only way to classify the majestic ages of some of those jokes was by geologic periods.

A Connecticut Yankee in King Arthur's Court

There isn't such thing as a new joke possible.
A Connecticut Yankee in King Arthur's Court

*

One is apt to overestimate beauty when it is rare.
Innocents Abroad

*

When red-headed people are above a certain social grade, their hair is auburn.
A Connecticut Yankee in King Arthur's Court

*

Nearly all black and brown skins are beautiful,
but a beautiful white skin is rare.
Following the Equator

*

It is human to exaggerate the merits of the dead.
Notebook

*

I do not make any pretense that I dislike compliments. The stronger the better and I can manage to
digest them.   "The Last Lotos Club" (speech)

*

It is a talent by itself to pay compliments grace-
fully and have them ring true. It's an art in itself.
"The Last Lotos Club" (speech)

Pity is for the living, envy is for the dead.
Following the Equator

*

[On war] A wanton waste of projectiles.
"The Art of War" (speech)

*

Thanksgiving Day originated in New England when the Puritans realized they had succeeded in exterminating their neighbors, the Indians, instead of getting exterminated by their neighbors, the Indians.
Mark Twain's Autobiography, Albert Bigelow Paine, ed.

*

Whenever you find you are on the side of the majority, it is time to reform.   Notebook

*

Necessity knows no law.   *The Innocents Abroad*

*

Necessity is the mother of "taking chances."
Roughing It

*

What then is the true gospel of consistency? Change.   "Consistency" (speech)

*

The man with a new idea is a crank until the idea succeeds.   *Following the Equator*

It is easier to stay out than get out.

Following the Equator

*

Thunder is good, thunder is impressive; but it is the lightning that does the work.   Letter

*

I would rather have my ignorance than another man's knowledge, because I have got so much more of it.   Letter

*

July 4th. Statistics show that we lose more fools on this day than in all the other days of the year put together. This proves, by the number left in stock, that one Fourth of July per year is now inadequate, the country has grown so.   *Pudd'nhead Wilson*

*

I have told him all about it. And now he knows nothing about it himself.

"The Begum of Bengal" (speech)

*

Prophecy: Two bull's eyes out of a possible million.   *More Maxims of Mark*, Merle Johnson, ed.

*

It isn't so astonishing, the number of things that I can remember, as the number of things I can remember that aren't so.

Mark Twain: A Biography , Albert Bigelow Paine

I must have a prodigious quantity of mind; it takes me as much as a week sometimes to make it up.
Innocents Abroad

*

I cannot keep from talking, even at the risk of being instructive.   "London" (speech)

*

I like a good story well told. That is the reason I am sometimes forced to tell them myself.
"The Watermelon" (speech)

*

I never had the courage to talk across a long, narrow room. I should be at the end of the room facing the audience. . . . You ought never to have any part of the audience behind you; you never can tell what they are going to do.   "Courage" (speech)

*

The idea that no gentleman ever swears is all wrong; he can swear and still be a gentleman if he does it in a nice and benevolent and affectionate way.   Taxes and Morals (speech)

*

When it comes down to pure ornamental cursing, the native American is gifted above the sons of men.   *Roughing It*

Constellations have always been troublesome things to name. If you give one of them a fanciful name, it will always refuse to live up to it; it will always persist in not resembling the thing it has been named for.   *Following the Equator*

*

It is your human environment that makes climate.   *Following the Equator*

*

The holy passion of Friendship is of so sweet and steady and loyal and enduring a nature that it will last through a whole lifetime, if not asked to lend money.   *Pudd'nhead Wilson*

*

You can straighten a worm, but the crook is in him and only waiting.
                    More Maxims of Mark, Merle Johnson, Ed.

*

It takes your enemy and your friend, working together, to hurt you to the heart; the one to slander you and the other to get the news to you.
                    Following the Equator

*

To succeed in other trades, capacity must be shown; in the law, concealment of it will do.
                    Following the Equator

I believe you keep a lawyer. I have always kept a lawyer, too, though I have never made anything out of him.   "Author's Club" (speech)

*

Few of us can stand prosperity—another man's I mean.   *Following the Equator*

*

There isn't anything you can't stand, if you are only born and bred to it.
          A Connecticut Yankee in King Arthur's Court

*

We have no thoughts of our own, no opinions of our own: they are transmitted to us, trained into us.
          A Connecticut Yankee in King Arthur's Court

*

Unexpected money is a delight. The same sum is a bitterness when you expected more.   Letter

*

There ain't no way to find out why a snorer can't hear himself snore.   *Tom Sawyer Abroad*

*

Noise proves nothing. Often a hen who has merely laid an egg cackles as if she had laid an asteroid.   *Following the Equator*

He is useless on top of the ground; he ought to be under it, inspiring the cabbages.

Pudd'nhead Wilson

*

Put all your eggs in one basket and—WATCH THAT BASKET.

Puddn'head Wilson

Bibliography

Quotations in this book are taken
from the following and other books:

Johnson, Merle. More Maxims of Mark. Privately
published, 1927.
Paine, Albert Bigelow. Mark Twain: A Biography.
Harper & Brothers, New York, 1912.
Paine, Albert Bigelow. Mark Twain's Letters.
Harper & Brothers, New York, 1917.

And the following works by Mark Twain:

Adventures of Huckleberry Finn. Charles Webster
& Co., New York, 1884.
Chapters from My Autobiography. North American
Review, September, 1906-December, 1907.
Christian Science. Harper & Brothers, New York,
1907.
Collected Tales, Sketches, Speeches and Essays,
1852-1890. Edited by Louis J. Budd. Library of
America, New York, 1992.
Collected Tales, Sketches, Speeches and Essays,
1891-1910. Edited by Louis J. Budd. Library of
America, New York, 1992.
A Connecticut Yankee in King Arthur's Court.
Webster & Co., New York, 1889.

Europe and Elsewhere. Harper & Brothers, New York, 1923.

Eve's Diary. Harper & Brothers, New York, 1904.

Extracts from Adam's Diary. Harper & Brothers, New York, 1904.

Following the Equator. American Publishing Company, Hartford, Connecticut, 1897.

The Innocents Abroad. American Publishing Company, Hartford, Connecticut, 1869.

Life on the Mississippi. Osgood & Company, Boston, 1883.

Personal Recollections of Joan of Arc. Harper & Brothers, New York, 1896.

Roughing It. American Publishing Company, Hartford, Connecticut, 1872.

Tom Sawyer Abroad. Charles Webster & Company, New York, 1894.

The Tragedy of Pudd'nhead Wilson. American Publishing Company, Hartford, Connecticut, 1894.

A Tramp Abroad. American Publishing Company, Hartford, Connecticut, 1880.

What Is Man and Other Essays. Harper & Brothers, New York, 1917.

The Gilded Age (with C.D. Warner). American Publishing Company, New York, 1873.

PLAYS

ELECTRA, Sophocles. 64pp. 0-486-28482-4

MISS JULIE, August Strindberg. 64pp. 0-486-27281-8

THE PLAYBOY OF THE WESTERN WORLD AND RIDERS TO THE SEA, J. M. Synge. 80pp. 0-486-27562-0

THE DUCHESS OF MALFI, John Webster. 96pp. 0-486-40660-1

THE IMPORTANCE OF BEING EARNEST, Oscar Wilde. 64pp. 0-486-26478-5

LADY WINDERMERE'S FAN, Oscar Wilde. 64pp. 0-486-40078-6

BOXED SETS

FAVORITE JANE AUSTEN NOVELS: *Pride and Prejudice, Sense and Sensibility* and *Persuasion* (Complete and Unabridged), Jane Austen. 800pp. 0-486-29748-9

BEST WORKS OF MARK TWAIN: Four Books, Dover. 624pp. 0-486-40226-6

EIGHT GREAT GREEK TRAGEDIES: Six Books, Dover. 480pp. 0-486-40203-7

FIVE GREAT ENGLISH ROMANTIC POETS, Dover. 496pp. 0-486-27893-X

GREAT AFRICAN-AMERICAN WRITERS: Seven Books, Dover. 704pp. 0-486-29995-3

GREAT WOMEN POETS: 4 Complete Books, Dover. 256pp. (Available in U.S. only.) 0-486-28388-7

MASTERPIECES OF RUSSIAN LITERATURE: Seven Books, Dover. 880pp. 0-486-40665-2

SIX GREAT AMERICAN POETS: Poems by Poe, Dickinson, Whitman, Longfellow, Frost, and Millay, Dover. 512pp. (Available in U.S. only.) 0-486-27425-X

FAVORITE NOVELS AND STORIES: Four Complete Books, Jack London. 568pp. 0-486-42216-X

FIVE GREAT SCIENCE FICTION NOVELS, H. G. Wells. 640pp. 0-486-43978-X

FIVE GREAT PLAYS OF SHAKESPEARE, Dover. 496pp. 0-486-27892-1

TWELVE PLAYS BY SHAKESPEARE, William Shakespeare. 1,173pp. 0-486-44336-1

All books complete and unabridged. All 5³⁄₁₆" x 8¼", paperbound. Available at your book dealer, online at **www.doverpublications.com**, or by writing to Dept. GI, Dover Publications, Inc., 31 East 2nd Street, Mineola, NY 11501. For current price information or for free catalogs (please indicate field of interest), write to Dover Publications or log on to **www.doverpublications.com** and see every Dover book in print. Dover publishes more than 500 books each year on science, elementary and advanced mathematics, biology, music, art, literary history, social sciences, and other areas.